Higher Ascension Tools

by Franziska Siragusa

Cover image: *'Oracle pink'*

Table of Contents

Introduction

I woke up one morning with a very exciting dream still in my mind. The Egyptian God Horus, one of my guides, was part of the dream. In the dream, we were talking about Egyptian treasures, more specifically 'The Treasures of Horus'. Horus revealed to me the first of these treasures with the word 'ciseaux'. This is a French word which I did not consciously know. When I checked with the Google translator, I found 'scissors'.

Interestingly it was the ancient Egyptians who invented the scissors. I realized that the first of these treasures was 'The Scissors of Horus'. In the dream, I was looking at a book. Am I supposed to write a book?

The next morning again I woke up with lots more information coming to me. It was clear now that Horus was definitely 'nudging' me to write a book and I was given the title 'Higher Ascension Tools' as well as the headings for all the chapters. I was also told to put an image of my ninth dimensional Diamond Unicorn guide on the cover. At this point, I felt much excitement, motivation and gratitude to Horus for starting me off on this project.

Note: Most of the time, I will refer to the Creator as Source although sometimes I might say God or Father-Mother God. I will refer to our Creator as he, but I think of him as both a masculine and feminine energy. You might have a different name for our Creator, which is also perfect.

Chapter 1

The Treasures of Horus

Everyone has heard about Horus, son of Isis and Osiris, an Egyptian God often shown as a falcon, or a man with a falcon head. Horus was worshipped in ancient Egypt but has been around for much longer than that. He was a powerful Atlantean high priest. Horus is an important guide to me, and I know we have worked together in several past lives. He has revealed two of his treasures to be included in this book, the 'Scissors of Horus' and the 'Atlantean Skull of Horus'. I suspect in time he will reveal more of them. Whatever his plan, I will go along with it.

The Scissors of Horus

The Scissors of Horus is a very special Ascension tool kept in a secret place within the Halls of Amenti. The Halls of Amenti are a sacred high vibrational space where time does not exist, past, present and future are one. Cosmic wisdom is stored here at different dimensional and vibrational levels. The space is guarded and whether access is granted depends on your level of evolution and must be earned. If you are reading this, you are probably in this position because of who you are and the level of mastery that you have reached in this life or other lifetimes, on this plane of existence or others.

Scissors symbolize the cutting and letting go of what no longer serves us. We all know how important it is to let go of the 'old'. The 'old' can be attitudes and beliefs that hold us back. It can be attachments to physical objects or even people. Once we let go and eliminate the 'old', we make space for the 'new' to enter our life. The 'new' is usually something better which brings us onto a higher path with exciting opportunities. We are in a constant cycle of releasing things and replacing them with something different.

However, the Scissors of Horus have a much more specific function. They literally help you to release you from the world of illusions that you have surrounded yourself with. What you see in your outer world, reflects your inner world. How can you distinguish truth from illusion? If what you see is beautiful and brings you joy and peace, then that is truth. If you see suffering, have worries and fearful thoughts, then that is illusion.

VISUALIZATION TO FREE YOURSELF WITH THE SCISSORS OF HORUS

1. Close your eyes and relax. Ground yourself by visualizing strong roots growing into the centre of the Earth.

2. Imagine yourself standing in front of the Great Sphinx of Giza accompanied by your Guardian Angel.

3. See a door of light opening in its chest, the heart area, and feel yourself gently lifted by your Angel.

4. Horus is meeting you at the entrance and welcomes you warmly. Ask permission to enter.

5. Horus raises his right hand and touches your Heart chakra to light it up at a higher frequency.

6. He touches your Third Eye and lights it up. Feel it tingle with a higher frequency as it opens up.

7. Horus is now granting you access, and you follow him into the tunnels of light within the Great Sphinx.

8. You are descending through tunnels and passages until you get to a vast high-frequency space. You see doors and guards.

9. Horus leads you now to the entrance of the 'Chamber of the Scissors'. He touches the door, and it opens magically. You see the special Scissors in front of you on an altar. They are glowing with an ethereal light.

10. Horus ceremoniously picks them up and sounds forth his powerful voice to ask you 'Are you ready to let go of the world of illusions that you have created around yourself?'

11. You say 'yes I am'. See or sense him cutting the energetic thread that keeps you attached to that world and note your sensations.

12. Follow Horus out of the 'Chamber of the Scissors' and follow him back up to through the lighted tunnels. Thank him with all your heart and soul before exiting the door of light of the Great Sphinx.

13. Return safely into the space where you started and feel grounded.

The Atlantean Skull of Horus

I have visited in sleep state and meditation numerous times the Temple of Horus in Atlantis. The temple holds a powerful crystal skull, the Atlantean Skull of Horus. I remember, on one occasion, I was accompanied by Isis through beautiful nature to the temple entrance. It all felt very familiar to me. I was invited in by Horus to visit the Skull and download wisdom. That was a special moment and privilege.

Horus wants us to know that we all have permission to visit and access what we are ready for and bring it back to be anchored and to raise the vibrations on Earth. The Skull of Horus is a very powerful Ascension tool. The visualization which Horus has given me to include here is very particular. You travel through the eye of the Skull, and you go back to the moment of the creation of your Monad to restore the right way of thinking and the right way of feeling.

The Monadic Family

Your Monad is your connection with Source. In the beginning, Source created divine sparks which are called Monad, or I AM Presence. The Monad is your highest dimensional aspect. To expand creation, the Monad has sent forth 12 Souls. This means you have 11 Soul brothers and sisters. To expand further, each Soul sent forth 12 extensions, one of which is your Personality here on Earth. So you could say that you have 143 cousins. This makes up your monadic family of 144. Depending on where you are on your spiritual path and with your initiations, you are guided by your Soul and Monad.

VISUALIZATION TO VISIT THE ATLANTEAN SKULL OF HORUS

1. Close your eyes and relax. Ground yourself by visualizing strong roots growing into the centre of the Earth.

2. Imagine yourself crossing a bridge that takes you across space and time to ancient Atlantis.

3. The Goddess Isis is waiting for you. Take a moment to embrace her and bask in her loving energies.

4. She is taking you on a path through wild, exuberant nature to the Temple of Horus.

5. Enter and find yourself standing before Horus who greets you warmly.

6. Horus touches your heart chakra to open and expand it with a higher frequency. He then touches your Third Eye, which also opens and expands.

7. You are now ready and have permission to access the Holy of Holies of this Temple.

8. You are standing in front of an altar with the Skull resting upon it. The Skull acknowledges your presence by lighting up and emitting a sound that matches the vibration of your divine essence.

9. The Skull speaks and invites you to look into his eyes. See or feel your spirit floating through the eye socket as it becomes a portal to a distant era.

10. You find yourself in the starry skies of the cosmos. You feel the presence of the Falcon God and see him flying with you.

11. He is helping you to access the very special moment when your Monad was created.

12. Pray to Source to restore the state of purity and innocence of this moment to you. Sense Source breathing into your mind, lighting it up and restoring the beautiful

high vibrational thoughts which he/she put there in the beginning. Sense how the breath of Source is re-energizing them.

13. Sense Source breathing into your heart, restoring pure love as was there in the beginning. Sense how the breath of Source is re-energizing your heart.

14. Take a moment to bathe in these beautiful energies.

15. It is time to return. Hold on to the Falcon God Horus and fly back safely through the eye portal of the Skull and find yourself back in the temple in front of the altar.

16. Express your deepest gratitude for this opportunity and the grace that you have received.

17. Return safely into the space where you started this visualization and feel grounded. You may wish to record your insights.

Chapter 2

The Seven Diamond Unicorn Ladies

Unicorns are radiant white superior beings, like Angels. They are pure and vibrate on a high frequency. Like Angels, they reside from the seventh dimension upwards. Unicorns tune into your Soul and help you to align with your Soul's intentions. They guide you onto your Soul path and into your mission. You know that you are living your mission when what you do brings you joy and satisfaction. Unicorns are attracted to people who have a desire to serve the divine with a pure heart. As you purify and evolve, they will come to you. The purer you are, the more profound will your connection become. Unicorns have a spiralling horn that protrudes from their Third Eye. They radiate purity and can apply their spiralling horn energy for healing. They can help you to illuminate your mind with truth. There are many Unicorns on Earth now assisting humanity and the planet with Ascension.

It is very easy to connect with Unicorns, all you have to do is think about them. You can have a Unicorn just as you can have a Guardian Angel. Although, your Unicorn guide might change and you might eventually get several different ones assisting you with different tasks. I worked for years with an elderly and very wise Unicorn with masculine energy, until one day when I was teaching a course on Atlantis a different Unicorn stepped forward and presented himself as my Atlantean Unicorn. I was very pleasantly surprised. This Unicorn is much bigger and exudes great power. Then more recently a beautiful feminine Unicorn stepped forward introducing herself as a ninth dimensional Diamond Unicorn, called Sarah. What struck me most about my new Unicorn guide was her beauty, her grace and the immense love she exudes. She has a white, lustrous long mane decorated with sparkling diamonds. She looks as if she had just got herself an exquisite hairdo for a special occasion.

I have written this visualization for you to meet your personal Unicorn, communicate with him or her, see what they look like and get their name. Your personal Unicorn will then accompany you in a further visualization to meet the Diamond Unicorns.

VISUALIZATION TO MEET YOUR PERSONAL UNICORN

Note: I will refer to the Unicorn as 'he' although you may perceive your personal Unicorn as a male or female presence.

1. Close your eyes and relax.

2. Call forth pure white Unicorn light and see it filling your space as it sparkles and glitters with golden and silvery stars all around you.

3. Breathe this light in and out; visualize it filling your aura as you continue to breathe in and out.

4. Imagine that you are walking on a path in a magical winter forest. Thick snow is covering the ground like a blanket, and the branches of the trees are laden with snow.

5. You are now approaching a clearing with a little flowing stream of pure water. You might notice animals like squirrels, rabbits, or even deer in the midst of trees. You feel safe and warm in this magical winter land and uplifted by the peace and beauty around you.

6. You sense a movement from the trees, and you see a radiant white Unicorn approaching.

7. He comes closer and stands quietly, looking at you lovingly with his gentle eyes.

8. Take a moment to look into his eyes and feel his love washing over you. You may touch and caress him. Feel your connection with him from Soul to Soul. As you feel his essence, you may 'remember' him from other lifetimes or other planes of existence.

9. Ask your Unicorn what it would like to be called … accept the first name that drops into your mind. This is the name which your Unicorn wants you to call him.

10. Your Unicorn is now inviting you to have a ride on his back. With facility, you climb up and enjoy galloping through the winter woods feeling free and full of joy.

11. Your Unicorn takes you to the path where you started your journey as it is time for you to return. You climb down from your Unicorn, and before he goes back into the woods, he may give you a message. Open up to receive it … it might be an image, a symbol, a word or a phrase.

12. Take time to thank your Unicorn and bring yourself back in the space where you started your visualization. Ground yourself by visualizing big roots that connect you with the centre of the Earth.

13. Open your eyes, knowing that you can now connect with your Unicorn anytime you want.

I learnt from my ninth dimensional Unicorn Sarah that Diamond Unicorns work with Archangel Gabriel, the Angel of Purity, to bring the divine quality of 'purity' to mankind. The Diamond Unicorns Temple of light from which they operate is located on Mount Shasta. Priestesses serve in this temple with the Unicorns, and they use special diamonds to cut away old belief, fears, illusions or anything else that no longer serves you on your higher path. They are called Diamond Priestesses.

I was given the title for this chapter 'The Seven Diamond Unicorn ladies' before knowing anything about the other six. Sarah then gave me the information that she collaborates with six other Unicorns and that they form a healing group of seven with a very special task. It is their mission to help you heal all that needs to be healed so that you can full merge with your Soul and blaze forth its highest light. I intuitively felt that there must be a reason why there were seven Unicorns working together in this group, so I asked Sarah. She responded that seven is the number that reveals truth and truth heals.

What does it mean to merge with your Soul or to become one with your Soul? Technically this happens when you reach the appropriate level of evolution, carry the required quantity of light, and have passed the necessary initiations. It is the third initiation that allows you to consciously embody you Soul and to radiate its light.

The Seven Levels of Initiation

To embark on a spiritual journey, you first have to step onto the Probation Path and become a disciple. This is a time for getting to know yourself and for building the causal body, which is your soul body. Then you move on to the Path of Initiation and are taught by initiates of the Ascended Master under whose care you are. Once you have
18

reached a certain level of initiation, you will have people under your care. To become a fully established Ascended Master, you have to take seven initiations with seven sublevels which you have to pass to complete the initiation. So for example, when you start your third initiation, which is also called the 'transfiguration', you then have seven levels to go before you complete it. After completion, you are a third level initiate and embark on the fourth level, and so on. Each initiation brings you an expansion of consciousness and information will be downloaded into you. How long you take for each initiation depends on your soul choices, karma and your determination to evolve. Discipline is very important, and as you probably realize as you read on, initiations can take many years and are major achievements. On the inner planes, there will be a ceremony where you receive the Rod of Initiation, take an oath and receive a gift. Djwhal Khul tells us that Jesus incarnated to 'demonstrate' quickly in one lifetime the first five initiations. In the life of Jesus and in Christian terminology, the first five are referred to as birth, baptism, transfiguration, crucifixion and resurrection.

First Initiation (Birth)

The first initiation is about developing a level of mastery over your physical body. You have to learn how to take good care of your body and to purify it. You have to listen to its needs in all respects, providing it with adequate sleeping patterns, exercise and nutrition. A high-frequency physical body will need high-frequency physical food. You may be tested with addictions to food, alcohol or drugs. You may need braces to correct your teeth, or you may need surgery. You may be asked to look into alternative methods of healing rather than traditional ones. When you pass this level, you have mastered the physical plane.

Second Initiation (Baptism)

The second initiation is about developing a level of mastery over your emotional body. This is where your emotions reside. When you have passed the second level initiations, you are no longer driven by lower emotions (anger, guilt, shame, jealousy, and so on). You learn to transmute them and to see situations from a higher perspective. You will have worked to heal your relationships and to forgive people. You won't get depressed or bored. The level of mastery is up to a certain degree, it does not have to be perfect. You can tell that you are working on this initiation when you are dealing with challenges in your relationships, your love life and intimacy. It will help you during this time of purifying your emotional body to watch only positive and happy programs on television. You are soul aware to some extent at this stage. When you pass this level, you have mastered astral plane.

Third Initiation (Transfiguration)

The third initiation is about purifying and developing a level of mastery over your mental body, again, this does not have to be perfect. The mental body is where your thoughts reside. You will realize that your mind, conscious and subconscious, is a very powerful tool which you need to put in use for mastering your emotional body. You do this by becoming a very positive person. You train yourself to have thoughts that manifest good things into your life and move you forward. You have to learn to observe and be vigilant of your thoughts and use positive affirmations to reprogram your conscious and subconscious mind. During this time, you may work at healing your heart and opening it more fully.

When you go through the third level initiations, you are very much aware of your soul, and your desire to be of service. You probably have embarked on your mission to some extent or are training for it. You have spiritual goals, and you are deepening your relationship with yourself and with Source. Your manifestation power is increasing. When you have completed this initiation you will experience what is called the **'Soul merge'**. This means that you now fully embody your Soul here on Earth and people will notice your beautiful light. You now have access to your Soul gifts and talents, and you are using them. On the inner planes, this is considered the first major initiation. When you pass this level, you have mastered the mental plane, and this allows you to choose your feelings.

Fourth Initiation (Crucifixion)

At the fourth initiation your causal body (soul body) dissolves and merges back into your Buddhic body (spiritual body). This initiation attunes you to your Monad, and you start merging back into it. This means you have now access to the guidance of your Monad who becomes your teacher.

This initiation is also called the 'renunciation' or 'crucifixion' because you are required to let go of any attachments and crucify your lower nature. You might have to take risks and a leap of faith. You may be required to leave a job, or work part-time, in order to start doing what you really like. Maybe you have to leave a relationship which is holding you back. You may need to make room in your life so that you can be truly yourself. You may need to study or upgrade your skills. As you go through this initiation you are anchoring your spiritual wisdom more and more, which allows you to make a bigger impact on more people. This is probably a very exciting time for you, and you are called to take action.

As you enter more and more into your mission, you will experience more abundance and joy in your life. Divine service is your priority, and you have access to your monadic gifts and talents. According to Djwhal Khul upon completion of this initiation you are free from the wheel of rebirth. If you come back, it is voluntarily because you wish to serve. When you pass this level, you have mastered the Buddhic plane.

Fifth Initiation (Resurrection)

The fifth initiation is also called the Monadic Merge because upon completion, you embody the consciousness of your Monad here on Earth at a deeper level, and you will have an even bigger impact on people. This initiation is also referred to as the 'revelation' and as the 'resurrection' in Christian terms. When you pass this level, you are on the atmic plane.

Sixth Initiation (Beginning of Ascension)

The sixth initiation is your Ascension, and you become a new Ascended Master. It is possible now to take this and remain in your physical body whereas, in the past, people would have left the Earth plane. In esoteric terms, this initiation is called the 'decision'. When you pass this level, you are on the monadic plane.

Seventh Initiation (Completion of Ascension)

You have completed your Ascension and are a fully established Ascended Master serving at cosmic levels. You can choose whether to carry on serving on Earth by keeping your physical body or whether to leave. In esoteric terms, this initiation is called the 'resurrection'. When you pass this level, you are on the logoic plane.

As you are only requested to master each level up to a certain degree, you can work simultaneously at perfecting all of them as you go up the ladder of initiation. So if you are working at the third level, you can still carry on perfecting the first and second level even though you have already completed them. And, you can already do preparatory work at your fourth level and the ones above, even though you are still completing the third level.

Some of us will have taken the initiations in other lifetimes, but we have chosen to reincarnate with the mission to help the planet and humanity to ascend. So we repeat them because the experience of working at them again helps us to transmit knowledge and wisdom to others.

Seven Steps to Align with Your Soul at a Deeper Level

So what can you do to be more conscious of your soul and to blaze forth its light and anchor it? I am giving you seven steps:

First Step

Remember that you have eleven soul siblings, call them forth, connect with them and ask them to work with you. Be aware that together, you have combined knowledge and wisdom to share.

24

Second Step

Tell yourself that you are your Soul. In fact, there is a powerful mantra from Djwhal Khul that helps you with that.

I AM THE SOUL

I AM THE LIGHT DIVINE

I AM LOVE

I AM WILL

I AM FIXED DESIGN

If you say I am the Soul, you are drawing towards yourself the energy and light of your Soul. 'Fixed design' means that your Soul is what it is. It is perfect, pure and divine with its unique qualities and mission. Nothing can change that.

Third Step

If you are your Soul, then you are feeling with the consciousness which is your Soul. Affirm 'I am feeling with the consciousness of my Soul.'

Fourth Step

If you are your Soul, then you are thinking with the consciousness which is your Soul. Affirm 'I am thinking with the consciousness of my Soul'.

Fifth Step

If you are your Soul, then you speak like your Soul. Before speaking, think about what your Soul would say. Affirm 'I speak like my Soul'.

Sixth Step

If you are your Soul, then you are acting like your Soul. Act in alignment with your Soul's will, which is in alignment with God's will. God is your heavenly father and loves you as his son or daughter. He always and eternally has your highest good in his heart.

Affirm 'I am acting like my Soul and my will is aligned with my Soul's will'.

Seventh Step

Have an image and name for your Soul. To help you do this, you are invited to do the visualization below.

VISUALIZATION TO HAVE AN IMAGE AND NAME FOR YOUR SOUL

1. Say the Soul Mantra and feel the presence of your Soul

2. See it like a radiant light ca. 20 cm above your head. Take note of the colour(s) and the form of this light.

3. The light is so bright that it dazzles your eyes.

4. Feel the light of your Soul descending upon you and integrating with your body. You might see it taking on the form of an angelic being as it merges and blends its body with yours...

Feel its heart merging with your heart.

See and feel its mind becoming your mind.

See and feel its mouth becoming your mouth.

See and feel its hands becoming your hands.

See and feel its feet becoming your feet.

5. Feel the light of your Soul spreading throughout your whole being and feel one.

6. Ask your Soul its name ... and open to receive an answer now ... accept what you are given.

You are now ready to go on a guided journey to meet the Seven Diamond Unicorn ladies on Mount Shasta.

VISUALIZATION TO RECEIVE HEALING FROM THE SEVEN DIAMOND UNICORN LADIES

1. Close your eyes and relax.

2. Visualize strong roots growing into the centre of the Earth and feel grounded.

3. Call your Personal Unicorn to your side and feel his loving and protective presence.

4. He invites you to climb onto his back, and you find yourself flying through the starry moonlit sky, across space and time, towards Mount Shasta.

5. You take in the breathtaking views of the snow-capped mountains and below you can see the Diamond Unicorn Temple shimmering in the Moon Light.

6. You are standing in front of the beautifully decorated portal now, and you knock.

7. A Diamond Priestess opens and welcomes you in.

8. She serves you a hot herbal drink which tastes delicious and energizes you as you soak in the ninth dimensional energies of the temple.

9. You tell the Priestess that you have come here today because you want to merge more fully with your Soul.

10. She listens attentively and asks you to follow her.

11. She takes you out of the main temple through beautiful crystal gardens onto a path that leads to a small healing temple.

12. Here the seven Diamond Unicorn ladies are already awaiting you; they know why you are here.

13. They ask you to lie down on a healing bed and instruct the Priestess to bring out a variety of sparkling diamonds which she lays out on a small white round table near you.

14. You close your eyes and full of faith and trust you surrender to the treatment. Your intentions are to let go of all the necessary to enable you to more fully access your Soul.

15. The Priestess works with the diamonds in your energy fields and skilfully cuts out any crystallizations that have formed to free you.

16. When the Priestess has completed her work, the seven Diamond Unicorn ladies step forth simultaneously and use their spiral horn of light to energize your bodies and fields with their magnificent ninth dimensional healing energy.

17. Sense and feel how the light flows into all of your bodies and into your chakras whilst you relax and enjoy the sensations.

18. Your body and aura are tingling now as the beautiful bright light flows through your entire being.

19. Your treatment here within this healing temple has come to an end, and the Unicorn ladies invite you to get up and follow them.

20. They lead you onto a path up the mountain.

21. You are passing a big majestic tree, its branches laden with snow. The first of the Unicorn ladies points out a sparkling magical fruit that you can easily reach. She would like you to eat this fruit. As you do so, she explains that this fruit contains a divine quality which is now packed into your aura. The gift that you have received here is the light of 'purity' which now flows through your heart and whole being and becomes firmly packed into your aura.

22. You walk on and as you pass yet another big tree, the second Unicorn lady points out another sparkling fruit for you to eat. She is offering you the gift of 'truth'. As you eat the fruit, you feel your Third Eye tingling and expanding; you feel your mind illuminating with truth.

23. You walk on, and as you reach the third tree, you are invited by the Unicorn lady to eat the fruit which allows you to increase your 'faith'.

24. You carry on walking up the path, and at the next tree, the fourth Unicorn lady invites you to eat the fruit which floods your heart with pure 'love' for everyone and everything.

25. You walk further up, and at the next tree, you are offered the gift of 'integrity' which is about acting with pure intentions. As you eat the fruit, this divine quality is being packed into your aura.

26. As you go further up you reach another tree and the sixth Unicorn is offering you the gift of 'power'. This power comes from knowing who you really are.

27. You walk up the last bit and on this tree grows the fruit of 'wisdom' which you are offered by the seventh Unicorn lady. As you eat it, you feel that your aura is packed with wisdom now, which you can access and use.

28. You have now reached the top of the mountain, and here at the very peak you sense and see the beauty of the consciousness, which is your Soul. With gratitude and joy, you merge … and the sensation of being one stays with you forevermore. Take a moment to enjoy this.

29. You are aware that you can now consciously blaze forth the highest light of your Soul and touch all that you encounter.

30. Take a moment to thank the Diamond Unicorn ladies for the experiences you made and for the spiritual growth achieved.

31. You notice that your own personal Unicorn is here too and feeling full of light and joy and peace you climb onto its back.

32. You are flying across space and time through the starry skies bathing in the loving moonlight until you get back into the space where you started.

33. You return safely into your body, and you ground yourself by visualizing big strong roots that connect you to the centre of the Earth. You open your eyes, and you are aware that you are radiating the light of your Soul now.

Chapter 3

The Powers of the Goddess

What is the Goddess? The feminine part of Source, represented by the many goddesses, Isis, Kuan Yin, Artemis, Brigid, Mary, Yemaya, to name just a few. Humanity is made up of men and women, and because we see ourselves either as a man or a woman we tend to do the same with Source, and as you know, he is usually seen as male. I believe Source to be the perfect example of integrated divine feminine and masculine energies, just as we should integrate and balance our divine and masculine energies.

At a higher level, we could imagine Source as a being of light, in the form of a shimmering sphere rather than a human form, with perfectly integrated divine masculine and feminine energies. If you take the human form away, it is easier to comprehend how masculine and feminine can be one. Your Monad contains masculine and feminine energies as one, just like Source.

The divine masculine energies are power, will, strength, courage, rational thinking; the divine feminine ones are love, compassion, intuition, wisdom, inclusiveness, caring, to name just a few. When you no longer perceive the God and the Goddess as separate, you reach cosmic heights. I wonder whether the language that is used to communicate at the higher cosmic levels distinguishes between he and she. I could imagine that they have a more unifying language.

The Goddess was well known and honoured in antiquity until in more recent times, the power of the Goddess was suppressed, and humanity has come to think of God as a male energy. This is starting to change now, and the Goddess is returning. Many lightworkers are aware of the power of the Goddess and are serving and working with her.

The Goddess has given me visualization for you to experience the light of your Monad descending upon you and showering you with the perfect balance of divine masculine and feminine energies.

VISUALIZATION TO MERGE WITH YOUR MONAD

1. Visualize your Monad as a sparkling golden-white light.

2. See it like a radiant sun floating ca. 40 cm above your head.

3. The light is so bright that it dazzles your eyes.

4. Feel its light descending upon you bathing you with power and love.

5. Know that this light contains your divine essence and perfectly integrated masculine and feminine energies.

6. Feel it spreading throughout your whole being and feel one.

The Goddess of the Oceans

One of the goddesses I particular like and have a connection with is the Goddess of the Oceans, called Yemaya. She is much celebrated in Africa, Brazilian and other cultures. She is known as Goddess of the living Ocean, Mother of All, Mother of the Waters, Mother Whose Children are the Fish, Ocean Mother, The Womb of Creation, Stella Maris (Star of the Sea) to name a few. It is said that she has created the sea, which is the source of all life; therefore all life has begun with Yemaya.

It is a Brazilian tradition to celebrate her on 31st December or 2nd February, and people will light candles, throw white flowers into the sea and make little votive boats which they cast upon the sea waters and processions of people are walking into the sea to give thanks. I have a permanent altar dedicated to Yemaya in my home decorated with an image of Yemaya, shells, mermaids, and other goddesses, and every day I light a candle to honour the Goddess.

I feel that my connection with this Goddess goes back to a very ancient era, Lemuria, where I was serving and working with her. I believe that at that time she was known as Ma Ra. My spiritual name is Laimara, this name speaks of the Sea as well as Lemuria, and it connects me with my essence, which is also that of the Goddess of the Oceans.

The Visualization that follows is service work to spread high-frequency love. You will be guided you to call down pure high-frequency love and send it into the oceans. You become a channel for it and send it to all aquatic creatures. All the waters of the Earth and indeed in the universe are connected, and therefore the love that you send will be able to spread and reach all there is.

The Antakarana

Before starting let me explain to you the Antakarana as you will work with this. The Antakarana is the bridge of divine light that connects your Personality, your Soul, and your Monad to Source. You can imagine it like a column of light that starts from the centre of the Earth, moves up through your chakra column, then up through the heavens and all the way to the Creator. It is your connection and keeps you anchored into the planet Earth and at the same time connected with the Source of your being. People who are psychic can see or sense this column which develops as you grow spiritually.

VISUALIZATION TO SEND LOVE TO THE OCEAN AND ITS INHABITANTS

Note: If you have access to the sea you can do this literally, otherwise just visualize that you are by the sea

1. Close your eyes and relax.

2. Visualize yourself on a beautiful beach.

3. Walk into the warm ocean water and feel it on your skin.

4. Connect with the Goddess of the Oceans and the consciousness that we call 'water'.

5. Feel yourself embracing the Goddess and merging with her.

6. Call forth the highest frequency of love that you can access.

7. See it descending through your Antakarana and chakra column right into the centre of the Earth to be anchored.

8. See it expanding through your entire being and send it into the sea.

9. See it reaching the whales, the dolphins, the sharks and all aquatic creatures.

10. See it reaching all people, in and out of the water.

11. See it spreading to all the waters on Earth and in the universe.

12. See all the waters lighting up with sparkling high-frequency love.

Working with the Goddess and the oceans, you will realize their incredible powers. Think of the ocean waves rolling in and out. They hold the power to transform. Water is a carrier for the energy we call 'love', and so are you. You can spread love. Water has the power to destroy, and that is necessary. The 'old' needs to be constantly destroyed so that a higher truth can come in. With the 'old' I mean that which no longer serves you and holds you back. Water brings so much to people and so can you. Water is the source of all life and brings abundance. It helps you to connect with the abundance in everything. The more service work you do, the more spiritual growth and abundance you will experience.

Like the Oceans themselves, the Goddess owns incredible feminine power and force. I have been given here to share with you a visualization to merge with the Goddess of the Oceans and bring her powers into your life. The visualization will bring transformation to you and make her powers also yours.

VISUALIZATION TO ACCESS THE POWERS OF THE GODDESS OF THE OCEANS

Note: If you have access to the sea you can do this literally on the beach, otherwise just visualize that you are by the sea. If you have a shell, hold it as you do this visualization.

1. Close your eyes and relax.

2. Imagine a beautiful beach with white sands.

3. Ground yourself by visualizing strong roots growing through the sands into the centre of the Earth.

4. Visualize yourself walking into the ocean water and feel it warm tingling on your skin.

5. As you look out onto the beautiful sea sparkling in the sunlight you see the Goddess slowly emerging from below the surface. She seems clothed with sparkling sun light, and she takes your breath away as you take in her beauty.

6. Connect with her as you slowly approach each other.

7. Merge and become one, feel that incredible love within her and within you, you are the Goddess now.

8. Feel the power of the Goddess flowing through you.

9. Command the waves to wash away the 'old' that no longer serves you. Make the power of destroying the old yours.

10. Visualize new exciting things coming into your life. Make the power to bring in the 'new' yours.

11. Command the waves to purify all your energy fields, and sense this happening. Make the power of purification yours.

12. Think of someone who needs help with transformation. Ask their Soul if they want to accept your help. If the answer is yes, visualize that person with you in the ocean waves, getting the help they need. Make the power of transformation yours; this is transformation for yourself and others.

13. Send pure love from your heart into the water and see it spreading to reach all there is. Make the power to spread pure high-frequency love yours.

14. Feel your heart leaping with Joy. Smile with the intention to share this joy with your brothers and sisters, for that is what they are. Know that your smile reflects how much the Creator loves you. Make the power to spread Joy yours.

15. The ocean reflects infinite abundance. As you are standing here in your power, as the Goddess; understand that you are connected with the abundance in everything. Take a moment to reflect upon this. If your eyes are truly open, you will see it and open up to it. Make the power of being connected with infinite abundance yours.

16. The ocean symbolizes freedom. Know that you are free of all limits. Make the power of true freedom yours.

17. Hold the shell in your hand to your ear and listen to the message which Yemaya has for you ….

18. Return safely into the space where you started this visualization and feel grounded.

Chapter 4

Expanding to Your True Cosmic Size with the Cosmic Whales

What Are Cosmic Whales?

They are immense whales of light. They have always existed, and they will always exist. They originate from a different universe. However, they are multiuniversal, and they can move across from one universe to another, by literally riding the universal waves. They are vast in size yet gentle and loving. Their task is to help with the Ascension process of this universe and all the universes. Just as humans, animals, stars, planets ascend so does the entire universe. The Cosmic Whales are the guardians of the universes and the cosmic currents.

They can help you with the expansion of your consciousness at cosmic levels. They are attracted to people who consciously want to work at this, and people who are willing to work at cosmic levels for the highest good. It is possible to visit them with your consciousness by simply setting the intention and with the power of your thought. They will welcome you warmly and will be very happy about you visiting them and working together. If you call

42

them to you, they will send part of their consciousness to touch you. This feels like a gentle breeze enfolding you lovingly. It may make you sway as it will immediately raise your frequency of vibrations and expand your consciousness. You may feel peaceful sensations like gently floating through the sea. Make sure you are grounded!

The whales here on Earth have incarnated aspects of the Cosmic Whales. They have come to show us how powerful we can be and how yet at the same time, love and gentleness are required. The blue whale might be the largest creature to have ever lived here on Earth. It can reach up to 30 metres in length weighing up to 144 tons. Their heart can weigh up to 450 kg, imagine all that love! Cosmic Whales have much larger dimensions and depending on the task they are carrying out, they can take on huge dimensions that span the universes. The call of the earthly whales is like a song, and in fact, people find it relaxing and buy CDs with whale sounds. The Cosmic Whales also work with the power of sound as they carry out their universal tasks. People generally feel attracted to whales, they sense how special they are, and that is why they go whale spotting or whale hugging.

Personal Experiences with the Cosmic Whales

I recently managed to manifest a new home for myself, after having tried for years it finally worked out. It felt like a miracle. I acted upon an idea, and within 3 days, I found a beautiful spacious apartment and someone to rent my smaller one. On the third day while awaiting the final confirmation from the owners I started feeling unwell and panicky. I knew I was letting go of something and I called in the Angels and Masters for help with transmuting the old that no longer served me. Then suddenly I found myself floating with the Cosmic Whales, big huge whales of light, floating around stars and planets. I was soaking in their light and energy, and I knew this was happening because my consciousness had expanded. I had passed this test or initiation, and the whales lifted me up onto a higher level. Later on that day, I got confirmation that the owners agreed for me to rent the apartment.

On another day I had a meeting at school about my son with all his teachers (he is a special child with special needs). As they were arriving and taking seats, I intuitively felt that I should call the Cosmic Whales to touch me with their consciousness. As soon as I felt their presence and my consciousness expanding, I reached out to touch all the teachers with my consciousness, sending them love. It was a great meeting, and everyone was really supportive.

VISUALIZATION TO HELP YOU EXPAND TO YOUR TRUE COSMIC SIZE

Note: If you have black tourmaline or hematite put it by your feet as you do this visualization. It will help you to stay firmly grounded. The more grounded you are, the higher you can reach with your consciousness.

1. Close your eyes and relax.

2. Visualize golden roots growing from the bottom of your feet anchoring you deep into Earth like a huge cosmic tree.

3. Invoke Archangel Michael to protect you with his deep blue sparkling energy.

4. Feel safe and secure and firmly grounded.

5. Call forth your 11 Soul brothers and sisters. Sense them arrive in the room and their consciousness joining yours, one after the other. Visualize and sense you merging with the first one, second, third, fourth, fifth, sixth, seventh, eighth, ninth, tenth, eleventh. Twelve of you are becoming one.

6. Imagine and sense all the wisdom accumulated on Earth, other stars, planets, constellations, even other universes. Feel the power of this merger and feel the expansion of your joint energy field.

7. Set the intention now to travel with your joint consciousness to visit the Cosmic Whales in their natural cosmic habitat.

8. The Cosmic Whales respond by touching you with their consciousness. You feel yourself lifted up through the dimensions, higher and higher.

9. Visualize yourself floating in the higher dimensions with big whales of light in the cosmos, in the midst of stars and planets, observing them as they ride the universal waves.

10. You now have the opportunity to connect with one of the Cosmic Whales. Sense his huge presence approaching and take some time to communicate with him and ask questions.

11. The Cosmic Whale is now starting to sing for you, and as you listen, you become aware of a brightly shining light. This is the Monad of the twelve of you.

12. Now visualize the joint consciousness of the twelve of you merging with the light that is your Monad. See and feel the Monad lighting up with joy and bliss.

13. Know that you are now accessing twelfth dimensional energy, and you are aware of your true cosmic size which spans the universe. Enjoy this for a moment.

14. It is time to come back from your travels. Take a moment time to thank the Cosmic Whales and to say goodbye for now.

15. Slowly start bringing your consciousness back into the room where you started this visualization, also bringing back the sensations and energies that you have gathered on this journey.

16. Bring your consciousness firmly into your physical body and feel its weight on the chair. Feel the contact of

your feet with the ground and visualize your roots anchoring you deeply into Mother Earth. Affirm that you are grounded

17. Start moving and open your eyes with a new expanded awareness.

Your True Cosmic Home

Each and every one of us has a true cosmic home. You have started off life somewhere in this universe or another. Your cosmic home is either the place where you first incarnated or another place where you had many incarnations and therefore feel at home. The connection to this place, consciously or unconsciously brings you happiness. We have all travelled far and taken on many tasks during our lives. Much time has passed, but time is just an illusion. Time is a tool to learn and grow. In your true home and in your true state of being time does not exist.

VISUALIZATION TO VISIT YOUR COSMIC HOME

1. Close your eyes and relax.

2. Visualize your big golden roots that keep you firmly anchored within the planet.

47

3. Think of yourself as the immense consciousness, which is your Monad and set the intention to visit the Cosmic Whales.

4. Feel their consciousness touching you and lifting you up. See yourself floating with the big whales of light in the cosmos surrounded by shining stars and planets. Listen to the song of the Whales and the sounds of the universe.

5. Set the intention to connect with one of the Whales and feel this happening. It may be the same Whale as before.

6. Ask it whether it would travel with you to show you the cosmos. Remember your Cosmic Whale can take you safely to another universe if it is for your highest good.

7. Ask your Cosmic Whale now to take you to the place which is your true home.

8. The Cosmic Whale starts to hum, and together you take off. You can visualize yourself on its back as you go on this journey.

9. Where has he taken you? What is this place like? What can you bring back from here? Let your consciousness take in the sensations and impressions that your Cosmic Whale is helping you to experience. Enjoy this for a few minutes …..

10. Take some time to talk to your Cosmic Whale; he may have some wisdom to share with you … then thank him for the journey that you have made together.

11. Bring your consciousness slowly back into the room where you started and then back into your physical body.

12. Take a deep breath to help you ground. Visualize your golden roots anchoring you deeply into Mother Earth.

13. Open your eyes and be aware of the sensations and information that you brought back with you. You may wish to record your insights.

Chapter 5

Aligning Your Will with the Will of Source

Setting the intention to align your will with the Will of Source is one of the most important steps that you can take on the Ascension path. This idea frightens some people, but there is absolutely nothing to be afraid of. Putting your faith in Source is the best insurance policy for a satisfying, happy and protected life. It implies that you believe and accept the divine plan that is in existence and that you work alongside the Masters to bring it about. When you align your will with the Will of Source, you know that only the highest good can manifest for you and for everyone, because Source, as any loving Father or Mother, wants only the highest good for his children.

The will you share with Source has nothing to do with desires and wishes that come from your ego, but is concerned with a higher level of wellbeing, that comes from your Soul. When you align your will with the Will of Source, you can easily achieve your goals, because they are also the goals of Source and the goals of your Soul. Your thoughts, words and actions will be accompanied by love, light and divine power. When you align your will with the Will of Source you are joining forces with the power of Source and the power of your Soul.

How do you know what the Will of Source is? When you listen to the voice of Source, you will know his will. There are two voices within you. Once comes from the ego and one from Source. The latter is usually quiet but it is there deep in your heart, and if you listen carefully you will hear it. So listen to the voice of Source and choose the path that brings you power, love, joy and peace that passeth all understanding. When your wills are joint, there is no room for doubts, because you will always know what to do, and it will bring to you what you truly want and what you have been searching for.

The First Ray of Power and Will

Source is beaming 12 divine rays down to Earth. The first three are called Rays of Aspect because they represent an aspect of Source. Rays 4 – 7 are Rays of Attribute because they represent attributes of God and Rays 8 – 12 are higher rays which can be used for world service. Each ray has a Master (or Chohan) and an Archangel associated with it who helps to direct it as well as colours. For the first ray it is El Morya and Archangel Michael.

Rays have a similar effect on people as the characteristics of the astrological signs, and they are also associated with certain professions which are influenced by them. Your Personality here on Earth is influenced by a particular ray, and also your Soul and Monad will have a ray which influences each of them. They may be the same or different.

The ray of power and will is my monadic ray which explains my affinity and connections with both El Morya and Archangel Michael. El Morya is one of my favourite Masters, and the Archangel Michael and his twin flame Faith are my favourite Archangels.

You could say that each ray represent a challenge, a lesson or initiation which once mastered leads to an expansion of consciousness. It is very beneficial to work and integrate all the rays, and you will find plenty of information about them. Much of the information about the rays comes from Djwhal Khul channelled by Alice Bailey.

For our work here we are concerned with the first ray of power and will. It is this energy that serves the purpose to align your will with the Will of Source and to step into your power. The colour of this ray is blue sometimes with red. It is the ray of leaders. It is the ray that clears obstacles.

The Ascended Master El Morya

The Ascended Master directing the first ray is El Morya. Being the Chohan of the first ray he is associated with power, will, courage and strength, which are divine masculine energies. He can, therefore, help you to align your will with the Will of Source. El Morya can also be associated wisdom and love. He had incarnations as a

52

number of wise kings such as Akbar, a Mogul emperor, King Solomon, King Arthur, and he was one of the three wise men, Melchior who brought gifts and teachings to Jesus. He was Shah Jahan who built the Taj Mahal out of love for his wife. El Morya has a message for you.

Channelled Message from the Master El Morya to You the Reader

Beloved Reader

Let me remind you although I am the Master of Power and Will, I have learnt to balance these qualities with love and wisdom when I was training on Earth. To serve a higher purpose, power needs love and love needs power. Add Wisdom, and they become a powerful and divine Trinity. Store this wisdom in your mind and heart and work to balance these qualities in you. Become a Master of Power, Love and Wisdom.

At your service, I AM El Morya

The Archangel Michael

The Archangel working on the first ray is Archangel Michael, the Angel of Protection, Courage and Strength. He is well known and much loved, and there are many churches dedicated to him. He is usually depicted as a Warrior Angel, holding the sword of truth and the blue shield of protection. He fights with love, power and wisdom and also truth. The image of Archangel Michael reflects that we are all warriors fighting our way through life's challenges. You can always ask Michael to lend you his sword to show you the right way and to cut away anything that no longer serves you. You can also ask him to lend you his shield to protect you. Archangel Michael is also sharing a message with you.

Channelled Message from the Archangel Michael to you the Reader

Beloved Reader,

It is with great pleasure that I take this opportunity to communicate with you today. As I connect with you feel a breeze of air gently sweeping over you, caressing you. I want to put your heart at ease and assure you that aligning your will with the Will of Source brings simplicity and lightness into your life. It will bring peace into your heart and mind. So take the journey with me to accomplish this step which will make your soul rejoice. Listen to how Source is rejoicing with you! Hear his laughter and feel his love flowing into you, into your heart.

I AM the Archangel Michael

Yours in service to the Most High

VISUALIZATION TO ALIGN YOUR WILL WITH THE WILL OF SOURCE

1. Close your eyes and relax...

2. See Archangel Michael coming into your room and start breathing in his majestic blue sparkling energy. It is filling and surrounding you … protecting you.

3. You are aware of your golden roots which grow deep into Mother Earth anchoring you firmly into the planet.

4. Archangel Michael sweeps you up into his arms to take you to a special place where you can experience and connect with energies of the ray and flame of power and will.

5. See yourself travelling through space and time with the mighty Archangel Michael to reach the spiritual retreat of the Master El Morya in Darjeeling, India. It is a beautiful building with towers and a central dome shimmering with sparkling white lights.

6. A gatekeeper lets you both in and takes you to the Master El Morya who welcomes you warmly. El Morya exudes power and authority, but he opens his heart to all initiates who come here with a desire to learn and to align their wills with the Will of Source. It is his job.

7. He leads you to a chamber with a comfortable chair and invites you to sit. Archangel Michael and El Morya are both with you.

8. As you look up, you notice that the ceiling is open and the most beautiful stream of blue shimmering light, you may see some bright red as well, is descending upon you.

9. Feel the light washing over you and filling your entire being. Enjoy this for a few minutes whilst reflecting upon your intentions and the concept of aligning your will with the Will of Source and deep in your heart and mind understand it.

10. El Morya and Archangel Michael now take you to the central point of this temple where on an altar you see the blue flame of power and will burn. You now have the special privilege to contemplate the flame and meditate for a moment.

11. Sense how the flame of power and will is ignited in your own heart. Visualize it burning away layers of illusion. See it becoming clearer and brighter now that it has been freed.

12. Visualize the same flame burning in the heart of Source. See a channel of light connecting you with Source and know that through this channel, you will always know the Will of Source.

13. You have a moment of time now to converse with El Morya and Archangel Michael, ask them any questions that arise and ask them to support you as you undertake this new higher path.

14. It is time to return. Say goodbye to El Morya and follow Archangel Michael out of the flame room and out through the temple gates. He sweeps you up again into his arms and across time and space takes you back to where you started your visualization.

15. Bring your consciousness back into your physical body, feel your feet firmly on the ground and start moving. Open your eyes and thank Archangel Michel for this enlightening journey.

Chapter 6

Accessing the Divine Thoughts and Emotions that Source Shared with You at the Moment of Your Creation

A concept from *A Course in Miracles* is that when Source created you, he shared his mind and thoughts with you. It follows that he also shared his heart and emotions with you. So your mind and your heart are connected with the mind and the heart of Source. Deep down in your mind are the thoughts that the Creator shared with you in the beginning, and deep down in your heart are the emotions that he felt and shared with you at that time. That particular moment of your cosmic birth was of course when he created your original divine spark, your Monad or I AM Presence.

What thoughts and emotions did the Creator share with you when you came into being? I will take you on a guided journey to the exact moment when your Monad was birthed and when the Creator shared his thoughts and emotions with you. You will have the opportunity to get your own personal insights, and I will also share mine with you after the visualization. You can easily access that point in time because, in truth, there is no time. Time is just a learning tool we have here on Earth, but in reality past, present and future exist all simultaneously, and you can connect with any point in time if you set the intention. We will call upon the help of the Cosmic Whales, whom you know from chapter four, as well as the Archangels Jophiel and Chamuel.

The Archangel Jophiel

Archangel Jophiel is the Angel of Wisdom and Illumination. He stepped forward to help with this chapter of the book because he is the perfect Angel to help you connect with the mind of Source.

Channelled Message from Archangel Jophiel to You the Reader

Beloved Reader,

I am the Archangel Jophiel

Greetings to you, my dear one. As you read this, feel your crown chakra widening and its thousand petals opening, like a lotus, allowing you to connect with a thousand divine qualities. Be aware of the inspiration that springs forth from this and the creativity that it unleashes. Therefore get to work and co-create with the Creator. Whenever you are in need of inspiration, just think of me, and I will start the flow.

I am the Archangel Jophiel

The Archangel Chamuel

Archangel Chamuel is the Angel of Love. He stepped forward to help because he is the perfect Angel to help you connect with the heart of Source.

Channelled Message from Archangel Chamuel to You the Reader

Beloved Reader

I am the Archangel Chamuel, the Angel of Love. I am the Angel that knows your heart and its divine origin. I am the Angel that can help you open and heal your heart so that you can fully love yourself, love everyone and see God. Call upon me, let me into your heart, and it will bloom like a beautiful white rose with soft touches of pink because I am the Archangel Chamuel, he who sees God.

VISUALIZATION TO JOURNEY TO THE EXACT MOMENT OF THE BIRTHING OF YOUR MONAD

1. Close your eyes and relax…

2. Visualize golden roots growing deeply into Mother Earth and anchoring you firmly into the planet.

3. Sense Archangel Michael coming into your space enfolding you with his sparkling blue protective energy.

4. Call forth the Cosmic Whales. Feel their consciousness touching you and lifting you up. See yourself floating in the cosmos with the whales in the midst of shining stars and planets.

5. Set the intention to connect with one of the whales and feel this happening. Ask the whale to take you to the exact moment of the birthing of your Monad. Remember your Cosmic Whale can take you anywhere, even on a multiuniversal level.

6. The Cosmic Whale is very excited about this mission. He sounds forth his song and takes off with you on his back. Take in the beautiful sensations and the high frequencies as you travel through the cosmos. Take in the beauty of the stars, planets, galaxies and all that you see.

7. Your Cosmic Whale has reached his destination, and you have the opportunity to witness the birth of your Monad.

8. You are aware of the loving presence of the Creator of your being. Open your mind, your heart and all your senses. As you observe the birth of your Monad, you may get images, sounds, or symbols, whatever it is take it in and treasure it.

9. Be aware of the presence of the mighty Archangel Jophiel, the Angel of Wisdom. He is helping you to deeply connect your mind to the mind of Source. Be aware that at

this moment, Source is sharing his mind with yours. You are thinking thoughts with the Creator, and they are being planted firmly and deep into your mind. Know that if you go deep enough, you can reach these thoughts. They are knowledge, and they are the truth. They are pure and divine. Open up to get insights of the most divine thoughts that reside and will always reside deep within you …

10. Be aware now of the presence of the mighty Archangel Chamuel, the Angel of Love. He is helping you to deeply connect your heart to the heart of Source. Be aware that at this moment, Source is sharing his emotions with you. You are feeling the highest and purest love together with the Creator. You are feeling the joy of a Father and Mother at the birth of their child. Know that this love and joy are being firmly planted into your heart. Know that if you go deep enough, you can access these divine emotions and express them in your life.

11. Take some time to take in more fully your experiences and allow yourself to remember who you really are …. Think about what you want to remember and bring back from this experience …

12. It is time to return. See yourself on the back of your Cosmic Whale journeying through the midst of stars, planets and galaxies.

13. Bring your consciousness back into your body, visualize your roots and feel firmly grounded. Open your

eyes and see yourself and the world from a higher perspective.

14. You may wish to record your insights in a journal.

My Own Insights

What did I feel with Source?

I see a beautiful shining white and golden sphere. I get the feeling that this is my Monad, and I identify with it, but I also get a sense of 'others' being there too, my monadic family. My Monad seems small, but only in comparison with the immense presence of Source within the immense cosmos. I cannot see Source, but I feel him. I get a warm feeling as if I am under a radiant sun. I feel as if I am in a cocoon of LOVE, and there is a big shift in the frequency of my vibrations. I feel very light, like a balloon floating in the cosmos. The LOVE feeling coming from Source towards me is immense, and it is a love that cannot be put into words. The feeling of being loved so much brings me immense joy and a great desire to share it. SOURCE IS LOVE, I AM LOVE, AND WE ARE ONE.

What did I think with Source?

I can perceive nothing except for love. The thoughts coming into my mind are these: Love shows the way to unveil truth and only love is real. In Source's mind, there is simply LOVE. Love is the key ingredient to my own creation and

63

everyone's creation. Love is the key to co-create with Source. Whenever I think, say and do something with love, it aligns my mind with the mind of Source. I now understand the saying 'God is love' because there is love in his heart and there is love in his mind. When I connect with the love of Source inspiration flows, and I can express his love into the world with all I do, my daily chores and activities, inspirational writing or talking, deeds and actions for the highest good of myself and everyone and the planet.

Writing this chapter and working with the tools it contains has brought me profound insights for which I am deeply grateful.

Chapter 7

Linking into the Consciousness of the Ascended Masters

The aim of this chapter is to make you aware that it is desirable to drop out of the mass consciousness and link into the higher group consciousness of the Ascended Masters. When you expand your consciousness, it is an opportunity to drop out of mass consciousness. The mass consciousness is what most people are part of. They just go along with everything and don't question much. They accept that things are as they are, and it may not even cross their mind that they could do something about it. This is the third dimensional way of thinking and living your life. In recent years humanity and the planet have evolved much, and many people are living in the fourth and fifth dimensions and can connect with much higher dimensional levels to access information and wisdom.

People living in these higher dimensions question why things are being done in a certain way and some move mountains to bring about change. They have a mission and realize that it is not desirable to be part of the mass consciousness. They will do what they can to help others realize this too. So what else is there available? As people

65

evolve and become Masters, they take control of their life and choose for the highest good. They are no longer part of the mass consciousness but part of the higher group consciousness of the Ascended Masters. At this stage, you no longer think of yourself as an individual, but you have the good of everyone in your heart and the planet's. 'We' becomes the keyword when you make decisions, and always take them for the highest good of everyone involved. All of us are on our journey back to Source, and complete ONENESS is achieved only when every single person has made that journey. This is why each person is equally important. We are all brothers and sisters learning the same lessons. We might be at different stages, just as our schools range from nurseries to universities.

The Ascended Masters are your older brothers and sisters who have had many incarnations here on Earth. They have learnt the lessons that were offered on this planet and are on their higher cosmic path of evolution now. They are, however, committed to teach us and help us move forward on our own Ascension path. The Masters have a spiritual retreat, a city of light, located in the ether above the Gobi desert: Shamballa. This is an important seat for the Masters to meet and take decisions. It is possible to visit Shamballa during meditation or when you sleep at night to receive teachings. Always make this request with love. You can use the wording below to visit Shamballa or any other spiritual retreat:

I (say name) have the intention to visit Shamballa in my sleep tonight. I ask the mighty Archangel Michael to accompany me and to keep me safe and protected on my journey. I am deeply grateful for the teachings that I am going to receive.

The steps that you can take to link into the higher consciousness of the Masters:

1. The first step is always to set the intention.

2. Focus your vision on being on a higher path and keep up your connection with the Master by communicating with them daily.

3. 'We' is the key. Have the good of everyone in your heart.

4. Think highly of yourself and affirm that you are a Master. This helps you to resonate with higher frequencies.

5. Think like a Master. Observe your thoughts and make sure they are aligned with divine thoughts. A Master has high, elevated, worthy thoughts.

6. Speak like a Master. A Master is always centred in love and speaks from the heart. So think first and say what a Master would say. Take higher decisions.

7. Visit Shamballa to receive teachings from the Masters.

Meet some of the Ascended Masters

A number of Ascended Masters have stepped forward to help with the work that we are doing in this chapter. To facilitate your connection with their energies, they bring you as a gift a channelled message.

Allah Gobi holds the title of Manu, which is a position in the Spiritual Government. He oversees the higher aspects of the first ray of power and will.

Beloved Reader,

I am a Master of power and will, and it is from the plane of the mind that I rule. My thoughts and words are clear and focused and aligned with the Divine Will of the Most High. Call upon me to help you focus your mind on the highest good.

I AM Allah Gobi

St Germain holds the title of Lord of Civilization, which is a high office, and his task is to oversee the founding of the new civilization of the Age of Aquarius, the new Golden Age. He has had many more incarnations than other Ascended Masters, and he achieved immortality. St Germain is connected with the seventh violet ray and the violet flame of transmutation.

Beloved Reader,

I am the Alchemist of the Alchemists. Life is a constant cycle of transmuting the 'old' that no longer serves us and embracing the 'new' that excites and motivates us. Call upon me to cocoon you with violet flames for your miraculous transformation.

I AM St Germain

Lord Maitreya is the head of the Great White Brotherhood and Sisterhood of Ascended Masters. He radiates the white light of purity. He holds the position of the Planetary Christ and embodies the Christ consciousness. It is his job to demonstrate and transmit this consciousness to you and every single human being here on Earth.

Greetings to you, my beloved Reader,

I get straight to the point. Know that you have got immense potential and I treasure our collaboration in manifesting the divine plan here on Earth. I know you, and you know me.

I AM Lord Maitreya

Lord Arcturus comes from the star Arcturus, which is the brightest one in the Bootes constellations. He travels on a spaceship called Athena. He has highly advanced spiritual technology available, and the Arcturian civilization is a prototype for the new Golden Age here on Earth. He works closely with the Ascended Masters.

Aloha, my beloved Reader,

I am the Lord of Arcturus. When you think of me, think of light because that is what I am and what I bring. Light is my gift to you. As you read this feel my light washing over you and your light levels increasing.

Aloha, love, peace and compassion to you

I AM Lord Arcturus

Mother Mary is a highly evolved being who was carefully chosen for her role as Mother of Jesus 2000 years ago. According to Diana Cooper, Mary is an incarnation of Isis. Isis gave virgin birth to Horus and Mary gave Virgin birth to Jesus. Mary's mission at that time was very important. She is known for her all-embracing and nurturing aquamarine energy symbolized by her blue mantle. As her name suggests, she is associated with the sea and the oceans.

Beloved Reader,

Although I have been given the title 'Mother' because I am 'Mother' to Jesus and to the whole world, know that the closer you get to me the more you will start seeing me as your sister, and you will join me in my mission to enfold the world in light.

I AM Mary

Lady Nada is known as the twin flame of Sananda. Sananda is the higher self of Jesus. She guides people to look from the perspective of love. This means you look at people's souls, and from this viewpoint, you will be able to remain centred in love no matter what. She taught me to pour love from my heart into the heart of others, paving the way for miracles to occur.

Feel my love pouring into your heart and expanding it. Throughout the day, do the same. Pour love from your heart into the heart of the people you encounter, every single one without exception.

I AM Lady Nada

Kuan Yin is known as the Goddess of Mercy and Compassion. She listens to every prayer and cry for help, and I know this is so, from my own experiences. Her energy is like the Tara energy, known for bringing release to 'the suffering'.

Beloved Reader,

See me reaching out to you right now. Feel my energy caressing you gently. Know that if you need me, I am there for you. Just call my name, and I will be right by your side to support you.

I AM Kuan Yin

VISUALIZATION TO VISIT SHAMBALLA AND LINK INTO THE GROUP CONSCIOUSNESS OF THE ASCENDED MASTERS

1. Close your eyes and relax.

2. Visualize strong roots growing into the centre of the Earth and feel grounded.

3. Sense the presence of a Master or Lady Master close to you. You may know him or her or you may not.

4. Together you are going to teleport to reach Shamballa. The Master is assuring you that you 'know' how to teleport as you have done it before. And so it is.

5. You have teleported yourself now in front of a golden, circular temple. It may feel familiar, as you may have been here before.

6. You enter and find yourself in a high vibrational hall of stunning beauty.

7. Lord Maitreya himself is coming to greet you and welcomes you warmly. You feel very special, and indeed you are very special.

8. He takes you into a circular chamber and invites you to sit. Explain to Lord Maitreya that you wish to step out of the mass consciousness and that you want to be part of the higher group consciousness to which the Masters pertain. Tell him about your desire to enter more fully into service

and to serve at a higher level... Lord Maitreya listens and is very pleased with your noble intentions.

9. Lord Arcturus, with a team of 'lightworkers', now enters the room. He is extraordinary and 'lightful'. Light exudes and sparkles all around him. With your permission, the Arcturians are going to use their 'light technology' to illuminate your mind.

10. Relax in your seat and feel your mind being flooded with extraordinary liquid light … You feel that something has shifted and your mind feels clear and light. Thank Lord Arcturus and his team.

11. Lord Maitreya takes you back now into the central hall of the Shamballa Temple where a group of Masters have gathered. They are greeting you. You may recognize some of them, amongst those present, are Allah Gobi, St Germain, Mother Mary, Lady Nada, Kuan Yin and more.

12. Lord Maitreya speaks and is welcoming you amongst the Masters. He is well pleased with your honourable intentions, and he offers you to undertake intensive training for 21 days in Shamballa. During your sleep time, you will have the opportunity to study and work with the Ascended Masters.

13. You feel very honoured, and with immense joy and gratitude, you set the intention for your Spirit to make the nightly visits.

14. You and the Masters are now forming a circle. Use your willpower to connect your energy fields with the Master on your right and then with the Master on your left. Feel how this uplifts you and know that your consciousness is now connected not only with all the Masters present here in Shamballa right now but also with the ones which are not. You are connected with all the Ascended Masters in the universe and linked into their higher group consciousness.

15. Feel the power, feel the immense love, and the wisdom that comes from this connection. You know what it means to be part of this higher group consciousness. Your keyword from now on is 'we'. And you also know, that even though you have opted out of mass consciousness, it is important to maintain your link with all of humanity, because your elevated thoughts will help to elevate theirs. You know that the fate of every single person on this planet is equally important, and every single one must make their journey back to God.

16. The Master who has accompanied you to Shamballa is now stepping forward again. It is time for you to return. Together you teleport back to the room where you started your visualization. Thank the Master for having accompanied you and wave goodbye as he teleports off again.

17. Slowly bring your consciousness back into your physical body. Start moving your feet and visualize your roots keeping you firmly grounded.

75

18. When you feel ready, open your eyes. You are smiling and looking forward to your nightly teachings with the Masters.

Chapter 8

Lifting Your Consciousness with the Planetary Logoi: Sanat Kumara, Lord Gautama Buddha and Adonis

Much has been written about Sanat Kumara, a mighty being, known by a number of names, the Ancient of Days, the One Initiator and the First Kumara. His home is Venus, and his twin flame is Lady Venus. He has been the Planetary Logos for eons of time, to be more 'precise' for 18 and a half million years. Despite his 'age', he is known for his youthful appearance. He took on the task or mission to become the Planetary Logos for Earth, at a time when it was considered a dark insignificant star. Stars and planets, just like us go through initiations. For a planet to reach a 'sacred' status, it has to pass its third initiation, which is the soul merge.

Sanat Kumara's act is also remembered as the 'Great Sacrifice'. The story goes that he sent out a 'Cosmic Call', and apparently people respond to this even now. He took with him 144,000 beings who volunteered to come to Earth on this special mission. It is said that he and Lady Venus were watching from their balcony when the 144,000 arrived. To continue the story, some of the volunteers went ahead to Earth before Sanat Kumara and built on an island in the Gobi Sea, which is now the Gobi desert, the magnificent and legendary Masters' retreat which is now known as Shamballa. This is how the activities for the planet of the Great White Brotherhood of Ascended Masters started.

In 1956 Sanat Kumara gave his post to his first initiate, Lord Gautama Buddha, who took on the duties of the Planetary Logos. Lord Buddha's incarnation as the son of an emperor is well known. He renounced his riches and family in order to seek truth. He found enlightenment at the full moon in 544 BC which is now known as the Wesak full moon. Sanat Kumara, from Venus, still overlights Buddha, planet Earth and those who have known him, know him and will always know him as Sanat Kumara.

What are the duties of a Planetary Logos? Being a Planetary Logos is a huge responsibility because he has to ensoul an entire star or planet. A Planetary Logos enfolds a planet and keeps the inhabitants in his aura and heart. The planet could then be likened to becoming his physical body. He takes on the responsibility for all the evolution on that star or planet, and the inhabitants literally live in his aura. On Earth, he is responsible for the evolution of all the kingdoms we have here: mineral, plant, animal and human. On different stars, this will vary.

How do you become a Planetary Logos? Sanat Kumara's teacher was a mighty Cosmic Master who wishes to be known as Adonis. Not much has been written about Adonis. He ran the schools on Venus where Sanat Kumara trained to be a Planetary Logos. Twelve training facilities

78

were built each with a specific function and tests. Joshua David Stone tells us that Adonis was considered the best at what he does, that he represents the heart centre of all existence and that he is the keeper of the Christ light within each soul. Adonis' theory was that if you can make your life work on a physical level, you can do so anywhere in the cosmos. Adonis is such a mighty being that he was able to teach two thousand students simultaneously and individually.

I have done much reflecting upon the tasks of a Planetary Logos, and I find it fascinating. Alice Bailey, in her book *The Rays and the Initiations* explains about the seven paths of higher evolution which a Master has to choose from to continue his cosmic Ascension. One of them is 'The Path of Training for Planetary Logoi'. If you feel very much attracted by this information, maybe this is also your path. As I have already mentioned, there are schools for the training of Planetary Logoi on Venus. Having learnt the technique, trainees have to pass tests. They learn how to be acutely aware of registering all soul reactions of all the inhabitants of the planet they ensoul. They are not concerned with individual states of consciousness but the **consciousness as a whole**. This reminds us again that we are on a journey here together with ALL our brothers and sisters, and it is love that holds us all together and moves us forward. We cannot go anywhere without the others.

Sanat Kumara had to learn to divide his consciousness into 900,000 aspects, and each aspect had to incarnate onto a different star or planet. The idea was to bring each aspect back into Oneness. Does this sound familiar? It is exactly what our Monad is doing. It divides into 144 aspects which then have to come back together. Sanat Kumara is doing this on a much larger scale.

As you can see a Planetary Logos is incredibly powerful. He has the special ability to lift the consciousness of the beings he is responsible for within a framework set by him. If you want to know more about Sanat Kumara's lives and training, I recommend that you read *The Story of Sanat Kumara – Training of a Planetary Logos* by Vyvamus, channelled by Janet McClure.

I have been guided by the three Planetary Logoi to create a prayer and a visualization which helps to accelerate the process for humanity.

Beloved Sanat Kumara, Lord Buddha and Adonis,

I pray and petition on behalf of all humanity to lift the consciousness of every being here on Earth to a higher level to accelerate the Ascension for Earth and all her inhabitants.

VISUALIZATION TO LIFT YOUR CONSCIOUSNESS

1. Close your eyes and relax. Ground yourself.

2. Sense the presence and light of Lord Arcturus in your space. He is going to guide and accompany you to Venus.

3. He invites you to repeat mentally the true name of Venus 'Eysmnje' (pronounce Ice-mon-ya) three times: Eysmnje … Eysmnje … Eysmnje

4. Feel yourself transported to Venus to the palace of light of Sanat Kumara and Lady Venus.

5. You are standing in front of Lady Venus. She dazzles you with her beauty. As she speaks a few words of welcome, you sense the immense love that radiates from her into your heart.

6. She is taking you to a balcony and points out to you the twelve training schools for Planetary Logoi. You see them as points of light in the beautiful, bright landscape.

7. Lady Venus is now taking you to one of these schools.

8. You are finding yourself in front of three mighty beings, Sanat Kumara, Lord Buddha and Adonis. They have been expecting you.

9. They stand around you now in a triangular configuration. Sanat Kumara in front, giving you the opportunity to look into his eyes. Lord Buddha on the right and Adonis on the left with the intention of lifting you into a slightly higher

81

state of consciousness that is safe for you and will accelerate your path.

10. Focus on your consciousness, and get a sense of the work being done on you.

11. Sanat Kumara now speaks and asks you to visualize your consciousness like a circle of light. He invites you to divide this circle of light into twelve aspects or fragments. See this happening and feel safe and secure as you do so.

12. For a moment, send these fragments out into the cosmos with the intention of each of them gathering some knowledge or wisdom which at this moment in time is of use to you. Visualize this happening … now mentally call them back. Do this with authority.

13. See the circle of light, which represents your consciousness becoming whole again.

14. The three Planetary Logoi now change places anti clockwise. You have Lord Buddha in front of you, Sanat Kumara on your left and Adonis on your right.

15. As you look into the eyes of Lord Buddha, you know exactly what to do now. You as an ambassador for Earth, petition him to lift the consciousness of all your brothers and sisters by a bit. You understand that Lord Buddha will assess your request and grant it either immediately or when the time is right and divine. Know that you have been heard.

82

16. The three mighty beings change places again anti clockwise. You find yourself looking into the wise eyes of Adonis. Sanat Kumara is on your left and Lord Buddha on your right.

17. Adonis takes you on a journey. With your mind's eye, you begin to see like as a slide show the most amazing places of beauty, they may be here on Earth, in this galaxy, in this universe or elsewhere. Just enjoy the show, let your imagination run ... You understand that Adonis, with his vast consciousness, is taking in all of this beauty simultaneously. He is giving you a 'taster' of how vast consciousness can expand and that this is the key to experiencing the beauty of creation and Oneness.

18. With all your heart, soul, mind and might you thank the three Planetary Logoi for the learning and wisdom you have received on your visit to Venus. Say goodbye, knowing that you can always come back.

19. Lady Venus is taking you back to her palace, where Lord Arcturus is waiting for you to accompany you safely back to where you started.

20. He is helping you to bring your consciousness back into your physical body and adjusts your aura to a manageable size. He reminds you of your golden roots that keep you anchored deep into Mother Earth, and you feel very grounded.

21. Thank Lord Arcturus and open your eyes with a sense of awe.

Chapter 9

Galactic Travel with Sacred Atlantean Cats

In this chapter, I would like to share with you an experience I had when meditating with a big apophyllite crystal. I visualized merging with the crystal, and it became a light green portal. On the other side, it was foggy, and all I could see was my bare feet and a black cat walking with me. I asked her 'could you lift the fog'? And so she did, and I could see that I was wearing a blue dress and I had long black hair. I found myself on a cliff at an incredible height looking down; it was so incredibly steep that it literally took your breath away. I focused on the cat now. She communicated with me telepathically, and memories came back to me. We were in Atlantis, and she was my temple cat Rora, short for Aurora. I was at the highest point of Atlantis, where the Temple of Poseidon is located. This temple housed the Great Crystal of Atlantis. This crystal is very powerful and an inter-dimensional portal. It is said to have sunk under the bottom of the Atlantic Ocean in the area of the Bermuda Triangle. I followed Rora through the temple gardens at the back of the temple, encountering more black cats. She led me up some narrow steps, through a back door, straight to the Great Crystal of Atlantis. As soon as I was near the crystal, I felt a powerful connection with the stars and was aware of my Merkabah lighting up. I knew that I could go anywhere in the cosmos, using the Great Crystal as a portal and travelling in my Merkabah. I took the opportunity and set the intention to meet with the Intergalactic Council. They received my cat and me in some kind of cabin in the midst of space and stars. I got the intuition that within this space they could receive whoever they wanted to and whenever they wished to. I had the opportunity to discuss with them a new task that I had been given, and they assured me that they were working with me, and I had their guidance in this matter.

Atlantean Cats

Often when I visited ancient Atlantis in meditation, I was aware of the presence of cats, in particular, black ones. The Atlantean cats were sacred and took part in ceremonies. I believe that it was the Atlanteans who brought this awareness and practice to ancient Egypt. Atlantean cats were held in the highest esteem and were honoured for the truly amazing beings they are. They were free and independent. They came and went out of their own volition. People recognized their power and gifts which they shared with those who cared for them. They had the special gift of being able to clear space and energy fields.

The Atlantean cats are still with us. Some of us have them as spirit guides, and others have them as physical cats in the home. They can choose to guide you from the other side or to reincarnate to be with you again. They usually turn up in unusual ways. I have learned that Rora is an excellent companion for galactic or intergalactic travel because she can keep my energies clear in order to facilitate the journey. Before I take you on a journey to meet your Atlantean cat guide, let me give you some information about your Merkabah.

The Merkabah

According to Joshua David Stone, we are all born with our own and unique Merkabah. The Merkabah is a body that surrounds our aura and contains our bodies of light. Our bodies of light increase in accordance with our personal evolution. This means that your Merkabah grows and changes shape and colours as you take your initiations and expand your consciousness. When we 'travel', either consciously in meditation or unconsciously in our sleep, we travel in the relevant light body and inside our Merkabah. I am going to take you on a journey now to meet your Atlantean cat, visit the Great Crystal in the Temple of Poseidon and take a galactic or intergalactic trip to a destination of your choice.

VISUALIZATION TO MEET YOUR ATLANTEAN CAT AND TAKE A GALACTIC TRIP

1. Close your eyes and relax.

2. Ground yourself by visualizing thick golden roots growing deep into the centre of the Earth.

3. Imagine that you are walking through a tropical forest with your Guardian Angel. You are arriving in front of a hanging bridge. You are going to cross that bridge in 8 steps to reach the golden age of Atlantis. Slowly take the first four steps, which will take you to the middle of the bridge. 1, 2, 3 and 4. You are now in the middle and can see the other side. Take the remaining steps, 5, 6, 7 and 8. You have now reached the other side.

4. You can see a beautiful and wise cat awaiting you. Take time to connect with her and for memories to emerge. You can communicate with the cat telepathically. Maybe this cat was part of your Atlantean household, or maybe she was with you at the temple where you served. You can ask the cat her name.

5. Before you move on, allow the cat to clear your energy fields. Sense this happening now, you might get a tingling sensation in your aura, and your frequency is rising.

6. Now follow the cat. She is leading you on a winding path up a mountain. The path may seem familiar, and along the way, you are passing a number of great majestic trees. Every time you pass a tree, you feel a shift in consciousness, and Atlantean wisdom is being passed on to you.

7. You are now reaching the top of the mountain. The view is breathtaking because you are at the highest point of

Atlantis. You can see now in front of you the Temple of Poseidon which is shimmering golden in the Sun.

8. The cat guides you to the entrance where a Priest or Priestess is awaiting you. You have special permission to see the Great Crystal and the Priest or Priestess is taking you there.

9. You are now in the presence of the Great Crystal which emanates incredibly powerful frequencies. You have permission to touch it. Do so now. You can feel an immediate expansion of all of your chakras, and you feel them becoming one single chakra column. You feel an expansion of your energy fields, and in particular, you are aware of your Merkabah. Try getting a sense of its shape and colours.

10. You now have the opportunity to take a galactic journey and your cat will accompany you. You may know where you want to go. Maybe to one of the planets or stars in our galaxy, such as Venus, Sirius or Arcturus. Be still for a moment and accept whatever comes into your mind. If you have clarity, set the intention to go there or you can set the intention to visit the place which can bring you the insights that you need right now.

11. See yourself inside your Merkabah of light, with your cat as a galactic guide, journeying through an open dome and a portal into the cosmos and reaching your destination very quickly.

12. Take time to take in your surroundings. There may be friendly beings of light welcoming you, sharing information and healing you.

13. It is time to return. Say thank you for what you experienced. In your Merkabah and with your cat, you travel back until you reach the Great Crystal again.

14. The Priest or Priestess accompanies you out of the temple and with your cat, you walk down the mountain, past the amazing trees until you get to the hanging bridge.

15. Take 8 steps across the bridge, counting backwards 8, 7, 6, 5, 4, 3, 2 and 1 and reach the other side.

16. Bring your consciousness back into your body, visualize your thick golden roots and feel grounded.

17. Open your eyes and bring back the experiences and insights that you gained on this journey. You may wish to record them.

Chapter 10

Being a Channel for Creating with Source

What does it mean to co-create your life with Source? We hear this phrase all the time, but how do you know that you are co-creating your life with Source? The answer is simple. You are creating with Source when your will is aligned with the Will of Source. When you think like Source, you create like him. Divine creation takes place when the Will of Source and you're will come together. The Will of Source is also the will of your Monad and the will of your Soul. So when the will of your Personality aligns with the higher will of your Soul, Monad and Source, divine creative power becomes yours, and you become a channel for the creation of Source.

How do you know that your will is aligned with the Will of Source? What is the barometer? You know it because you are happy and joyful. Your activities bring you satisfaction. You feel motivated and enthusiastic about your life, and you know your purpose. Your manifestation power is increasing, and you successfully manifest good things into your life. You are probably experiencing changes which are for the better. You see the world as a beautiful place and feel blessed to be here.

What you have in your heart is reflected in how you see the outside world. You might ask, but what about the 'bad' things happening here on Earth? You will know them as an illusion. Source is pure love, and all that is love comes from Source, anything else is illusion. What comes from your Soul and Monad is love. Anything else serves for us to recognize it as illusion, see beyond and grow. This does not mean that you do not care about what happens in the world, quite the opposite. Your positive outlook will help to eliminate illusion and make space for the new Golden Age to be firmly established for everyone.

A channelled message I have received:

The new Golden Age is already here if you want it to be. Look deep inside your heart, and you will remember and find it there. You can live in the new fifth dimensional era right now, just let go of all illusion and focus on love and beauty. With love and beauty in your heart, you will see and be surrounded by love and beauty and recognize anything else for illusion.

There are seven steps you can take to be a channel for creating with Source:

1. Set the intention to only see love and beauty, and to truly appreciate the world.

2. Feel blessed to be here on Earth and love your life.

3. Love yourself and all of humanity. Love minerals, animals, nature, elemental beings and the spiritual hierarchy.

4. Set the intention to only manifest good into your life.

5. Set the spiritual goal to evolve as much as you can.

6. Learn to separate divine creation and illusion: everything that comes from your Soul and Monad and from Source is divine and real, everything else is illusion.

7. Embody your Soul here on Earth.

What does it mean to embody your Soul here on Earth? Technically it means that you have passed your third initiation, as you know already. When you embody your Soul, you automatically are a channel for divine creation. You take instructions from your Soul. The objective of the next visualization is to help you understand what your Soul wants you to do and to take action.

VISUALIZATION TO BECOME A CHANNEL FOR DIVINE CREATION

Note: Keep a paper and pen ready to record your insights.

1. Close your eyes and relax.

2. Ground yourself by sending your big golden roots down into the centre of Mother Earth.

3. Put your hands on your heart and focus on it. Your heart is your inner kingdom. Visualize it like a magical castle or temple with beautiful gardens. Decorate it just how like it. Make it as beautiful as you can. Let your imagination run and decide how you want your inner kingdom to be. Know that your inner kingdom will be reflected in the outside world that you see.

4. Think of your Soul inhabiting your inner kingdom. Feel at one, be your Soul and communicate with it. Ask your Soul: What brings you satisfaction? Open up to receive information and let at least three things drop into your mind, accept whatever comes … (write them down)

5. Then ask your Soul, what action would you like me to take? Again open up to receive information and let at least three things drop into your mind … (write them down)

6. From the information you have received, intuitively choose the most important answer you got from each question. Highlight what stands out for you.

7. Bring your consciousness fully back into your physical body.

8. Take some time to take in and process the information that you have received and act upon it.

VISUALIZATION TO APPRECIATE THE CREATION
OF SOURCE

Note: If possible, take a walk outside in nature to do this.

1. Appreciate the beauty of nature, plants, trees and flowers. Think about the beauty of the oceans, the lakes and the rivers. Send gratitude to nature, to the waters and to the elemental beings who take care of it.

2. Send gratitude to the minerals, the crystals, the rocks and the mountains. They are conscious beings, and they are helping to raise the frequencies here on Earth.

3. Think about all your brothers and sisters. Look at their Soul and see the beauty of it. No matter what they do, they are on the same journey as you are with one single destination: Source.

4. Think about your brothers and sisters on other stars and planets and send them love.

5. Send your love and gratitude to the Masters, the Angels and Source.

6. Put your hands on your heart and bless all there is. Pray for yourself and for everyone to see only the love and beauty of Source so that the new Golden Age can manifest for everyone.

7. Set the intention to view the world from this higher perspective from now onwards.

Chapter 11

Training with Isis in Her Atlantean Temple

We all have heard of Isis who was considered a major goddess in ancient Egypt. She was married to Osiris and gave birth to Horus, the Falcon God which you have got to know at the beginning of this book. Like Horus, Isis was around way before Egypt. She too was a powerful high priestess in Atlantis. After the fall of Atlantis, many high priests and priestesses went to other places in the world, bringing with them Atlantean wisdom. Isis became venerated as a goddess in Egypt, and we often see her depicted with wings. The wings to me are a visual sign of her powerful, all-embracing and nurturing energy.

Diana Cooper tells us that Atlantis existed over a period of 260,000 years. So almost everyone has had at least one life in Atlantis if not several and very likely you have met other people which you knew in Atlantis. I have met several. In the Golden Age of Atlantis, I trained with Isis, and one of her teachings was this:

Use your power with love

I had visions and dreams of her embracing me and telling me this phrase. It was important for me to remember it in this lifetime. I didn't understand at the time the entire significance of this phrase as I do now. It is connected with the first three divine Rays of Aspect, each of them representing an aspect of Source. The first ray is of power and will, the second of love and wisdom, and third of divine intelligence. These qualities are important lessons and initiations here on Earth. We all have to learn to step into our power and at the same time, develop and increase love in ourselves. Power without love is not desirable, and love without power has no force. As you develop power and love, wisdom grows. Wisdom goes hand in hand with love because you can't be 'wise' without love.

Power and love are also the two qualities which describe Isis best. She is an extraordinary powerful goddess and at the same time so loving. I will share with you in the form of visualization some of the Atlantean memories I have. The visualization has the objective of connecting you with Isis and to receive a message for yourself.

VISUALIZATION TO MEET ISIS IN ANCIENT ATLANTIS

Note: Keep paper and a pen ready to record your insights.

1. Close your eyes and relax.

2. Ground yourself by visualizing golden roots keeping you firmly anchored into Earth.

3. Your Guardian Angel is by your side to accompany you on your journey. You are safe and protected.

4. Take yourself back far in time to ancient Atlantis, to the temple of the Goddess Isis. Many temples dedicated to Isis have been discovered in the world. This temple which you are seeing now is her own temple where she served.

5. See yourself standing in front of this temple and take in its glory.

6. Notice the sacred cats which are coming to greet you. You are connecting with one of them, and she is now leading you down a path through a tropical forest until you get to a clearing.

7. You have the opportunity to observe a gathering. Trainee priestesses are about to perform a sacred dance to honour Isis but also to honour a more ancient Goddess. Maybe you are one of these trainee priestesses, or maybe you are just observing them.

8. The music starts … feel the sound washing over you entering your cells … sense how your frequencies are rising. The dancers are dressed with blue flowing vests, and their movements are mesmerizing. They bring back memories of ancient Atlantis. Just relax and let them come to the surface (take a few minutes 'to remember')

9. The dance is finished now, and Isis is embracing each of the dancers and whispers something in her ear.

10. Now it is your turn. See Isis standing in front of you. Visualize her with wings as she is often depicted. She is embracing you now both with her arms and wings. Sense

the power and the love in this embrace. She whispers a message into your ear that has meaning for you right now… Thank Isis for the message you have received.

11. It is time to return. Follow your cat back on the path that you came. Bring your consciousness slowly back into the room where you started and ground yourself. Open your eyes and take notes of any insights which you may have received.

Chapter 12

Embracing Jesus

I was brought up with the Catholic religion and had to go to church every weekend as a child, and I did not like it. When I embarked on my spiritual path, interestingly my parents did too. I initially felt much resistance towards Jesus. I always felt that the other 'Masters' were underrated and didn't get enough 'publicity'. So I took on the 'job' to stand up for them and argue that they were equally as important as Jesus (which they are) and I focused on working with them.

This doesn't mean that I didn't like Jesus. Let's just say that I ignored him for while. He didn't ignore me though. At some point, I saw him very clearly in my room whilst I was in a dream state. I am claircognizant, so when I channel or work with masters, the information just drops into my mind. This means that I just 'know' who is present and what they want to tell me, rather than hearing or seeing them. So when I 'saw' Jesus, I was quite surprised. It stood out for me that I was given such a clear image of what he looks like. It then happened that I kept getting the message to embrace Jesus. This was a repeating message over a period of time until I finally did it.

It was an eye-opener when I fully understood what Jesus' mission actually is. Jesus' particular job is to make sure that we all make our journey home to Source. Let me explain the Trinity to you, the Father, the Son and the Holy Spirit. According to '*A Course in Miracles*' which contains channelled information from Jesus, the Holy Spirit was sent by God or by Source when humanity became separated, when we no longer felt one with Source. So the job of the Holy Spirit is to remind us of our unity with Source and to listen to his voice rather than the voice of the ego which supports separation. 'Son' is not just Jesus. The Son is all of us; we are all sons and daughters of God, and brothers and sisters to Jesus and to each other.

Jesus came as a way-shower. He showed us the right way of thinking and feeling. He showed us love and forgiveness. He showed us how to go through the first five initiations. Jesus is the light of the world, and so are we. It is our job to light up the world, just like he showed us. This does not mean we have to suffer, he has done that already. It means to embrace him, to take on the Christ consciousness and demonstrate it here on Earth. That's when the doors to heaven open for you, and you enter the kingdom of God. Taking on the Christ consciousness means to radiate unconditional love, preferably 24 hrs a day. Embrace Jesus as your brother and help him with lighting up the world. Accept that you are an incarnation of Source.

VISUALIZATION TO BE A CHANNEL FOR THE CHRIST LIGHT

1. Close your eyes and relax.

2. Send your roots lovingly deep down into the Earth to keep you radicated.

3. See yourself standing in front of a brightly shining golden portal.

4. Looking through the portal, you can see the figure of Jesus standing there.

5. He is smiling at you and radiating golden light.

6. He is opening his arms, encouraging you to cross the portal and to embrace him.

7. If you feel ready, do so now.

8. See and feel yourself embracing Jesus like a long lost brother.

9. You may feel emotional, you may feel deep joy.

10. Jesus is sending love from his heart into your heart, and you are sending love from your heart into his heart.

11. Be aware of how open your heart is right now.

12. Reflect for a moment upon the principal of the Christ consciousness, which is all about love and forgiveness. Decide consciously that you want to be a channel for the Christ light and to use it to light up the world.

13. Communicate your intentions to Jesus. Jesus is thanking you for taking on this noble mission.

14. It is time to return, so say goodbye to Jesus. Come back through the golden portal, bringing with you an open heart and a newly profound connection with Jesus and the Christ light.

15. Bring your consciousness back into your body. Start moving and open your eyes. Know that you are a channel for the Christ light and that you are working with Jesus.

Bibliography:

The Rays and the Initiations, Alice A Bailey, Lucis Publishing Company

Initiation Human and Solar, Alice A Bailey, Lucis Publishing Company

Discover Atlantis, Diana Cooper and Shaaron Hutton, Hodder Mobius

A New Light on Ascension, Diana Cooper, Findhorn Press

The Story of Sanat Kumara – Training of a Planetary Logos by Vyvamus' channelled by Janet McClure, Light Technology Publishing

We, the Arcturians, Dr Norma J Milanovich, Athena Publishing

The Masters and their Retreats, Mark L. Prophet and Elizabeth Clare Prophet, Summit University Press

The Ascension Manual, Joshua David Stone, Light Technology Publishing

A Course in Miracles, Course in Miracles Society

I AM University Training Course: How to Construct your Integrated Lightbody and Anchor and Activate the 22 Levels of Lightbody

You can find the Visualizations here:

Franziska is an international Spiritual Teacher, Author and Ascension Guide. She is a Principal Teacher with the Diana Cooper School of White Light, a not-for-profit organization that offers certified spiritual teaching courses. She teaches and writes about subjects such as Ascension, Atlantis, Lemuria, Angels, Unicorns, Cosmic Whales and the new Golden Age. Her universal name is Laimara which connects her to the Goddess and the ancient Seas of Lemuria. As a Priestess of the Order of Melchizedek she has taken on the mission to serve Earth and humanity. She is dedicated to help people to embody their Soul and to recognize their divinity. She feels honoured and excited about the opportunity of sharing her wisdom with others and to learn from everyone she encounters.

She has a great passion and connection with the ocean and its inhabitants, especially dolphins, whales, sharks, turtles, manatees and mermaids; they make her heart leap with joy!

I AM LAIMARA
I AM THE SEAS OF THE UNIVERSE
I AM COSMIC LOVE
I AM COSMIC CONSCIOUSNESS
I AM LAIMARA

www.angeldolphins.com